COOKING QUINOA

50 DELIGHTFUL RECIPES

BARDALPH GREEN

Disclaimer

The information contained i is meant to serve as a comprehensive collection of strategies that the author of this eBook has done research about. Summaries, strategies, tips and tricks are only recommendation by the author, and reading this eBook will not guarantee that one's results will exactly mirror the author's results. The author of the eBook has made all reasonable effort to provide current and accurate information for the readers of the eBook. The author and it's associates will not be held liable for any unintentional error or omissions that may be found. The material in the eBook may include information by third parties. Third party materials comprise of opinions expressed by their owners. As such, the author of the eBook does not assume responsibility or liability for any third party material or opinions. Whether because of the progression of the internet, or the unforeseen changes in company policy and editorial submission guidelines, what is stated as fact at the time of this writing may become outdated or inapplicable later.

TABLE OF CONTENTS

INTRODUCTION

What is Quinoa ?

Quinoa is a gluten-free seed that can make a great substitute for rice and other grains.

these days, quinoa is still all anyone talks about. Everywhere we turn there are quinoa salads, quinoa fried rice, and now even quinoa protein shakes. Forged in South America thousands of years ago and called "the mother grain" by the Inca, quinoa today is still considered a superfood.

But when and why did quinoa become so popular? What is it that makes this low-carb rice substitute so invaluable in the world of nutrition despite all the years that have passed?

Overall, quinoa has an incredible nutrition base. Compared with refined grains, whole grains like quinoa are considered better sources of fiber, protein, B vitamins, and iron, according to the Mayo Clinic. But aside from these key nutrients, one of the greatest nutrient profiles quinoa can offer is its level of protein.Because protein makes up 15 percent of the grain, as reported by the Grains & Legumes Nutrition Council, quinoa is a high-protein, low-fat grain option.

It's also naturally gluten free, high in fiber, and provides many key vitamins and minerals, including vitamin B and magnesium, lists the U.S. Department of Agriculture's MyPlate guidelines. Because it is so nutrient-rich, quinoa is a wonderful choice for people on a gluten-free diet or any generally healthy diet.

QUINOA BREAKFAST

1. Hot quinoa breakfast cereal

Yield: 5 Servings

Ingredient

- 1 cup Quinoa

- 2 cups ;Water

- ½ cup Apples; thinly sliced

- ⅓cup Raisins

- ½ teaspoon Cinnamon

- Milk or cream

- Honey or brown sugar

Rinse quinoa and add to water; bring to a boil. Reduce heat; simmer for 5 minutes. Add apples, raisins and cinnamon; simmer until water is absorbed. Serve with milk or cream and sweeten to taste with honey or brown sugar.

2. Red sage quinoa bread

Yield: 16 Servings

Ingredient

- 1 cup Lukewarm water; 105-115F

- 2 tablespoons Lukewarm milk

- 2 tablespoons Canola oil OR corn oil

- 2 teaspoons Active dry yeast

- Cooked quinoa

- ½ cup Whole wheat flour

- 3 cups Bread flour

- 3 tablespoons Dried rubbed sage

- 12 Fresh sage leaves; coarsely chopped

- 1 tablespoon Chile molindo

- $2\frac{1}{2}$ teaspoon Salt

Combine the ingredients, except the fresh sage, in the bread pan in the order specified by the manufacturer's instructions.

Process on the sweet or raisin bread setting

Add the fresh sage at the beeps.

3. Quinoa Breakfast Bake

Ingredients

- 1/2 cup quinoa uncooked

- 1/2 cup steel cut oats uncooked

- 1/4 cup coconut flakes unsweetened

- 3 medium very ripe bananas sliced

- 1 1/2 cups blueberries fresh or frozen

- 1/2 cup raspberries fresh or frozen

- 2 cups any milk I used almond

- 2 large eggs

- 1 - 2 tbsp maple syrup or honey

- 1 tsp pure vanilla extract

- 1/2 tsp cinnamon and Dash of salt

Preheat small skillet on low-medium heat, add coconut and toast until golden brown, stirring frequently. Set aside.

In medium bowl, whisk milk, eggs, maple syrup, vanilla extract, cinnamon and salt. Set aside.

Lay half of bananas, blueberries and raspberries in a single layer on a bottom. Using a spoon or spatula, spread rinsed quinoa and steel cut oats on top. Top with remaining banana and berries.

Slowly pour liquid mixture in the corner of the baking dish without disturbing the set up. Sprinkle with toasted coconut flakes and bake for 60 minutes uncovered.

4. Berry Quinoa Salad

Ingredients

Citrus Honey Dressing:

- 1 teaspoon orange zest

- 4 tablespoons fresh orange juice

- 2 tablespoons fresh lemon juice

- 1 tablespoon fresh lime juice

- 1 tablespoon honey

- 1 teaspoon finely chopped mint

- 1 teaspoon finely chopped basil

For the Salad:

- 2 cups cooked red quinoa

- 1 1/2 cups strawberries cut in half

- 1 cup raspberries

- 1 cup blackberries

- 1 cup blueberries

- 1 cup Honey Roasted Cinnamon Almonds

- 1 tablespoon finely chopped mint

- 1 tablespoon finely chopped basil

Instructions

First, make the dressing. In a small bowl or jar, whisk together the orange zest, orange juice, lemon juice, lime juice, honey, mint, and basil. Set aside.

In a large bowl, combine cooked quinoa, strawberries, raspberries, blackberries, blueberries, almonds, mint, and basil. Gently stir. Drizzle citrus honey dressing over the salad and gently stir again. Serve.

5. Quinoa Crunch Bars

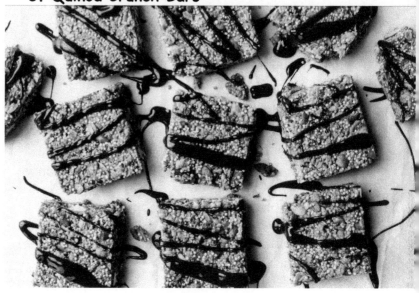

Ingredients

- 5 Medjool dates, pitted
- 1 cup whole rolled oats
- 3/4 cup (130g) uncooked quinoa
- 1/2 cup (70g) coarsely chopped almonds
- 1/2 cup (70g) pepitas (pumpkin seeds)
- 1 Tablespoon chia seeds
- 1/2 cup (125g) almond butter
- 1/3 cup (114g) honey
- 1 teaspoon pure vanilla extract

- 1/4 teaspoon salt

- 2 ounces melted semi-sweet chocolate

Instructions

Pulse the dates in a food processor. Add the remaining ingredients to the bowl (except for the chocolate).

Transfer mixture to prepared baking pan and press very firmly into an even layer. Bake for 20-22 minutes. Remove and chill. You can drizzle with chocolate before or after cutting.

6. Quinoa Breakfast Cookies

Ingredients

- 1 cup oat flour

- 1 cup whole rolled oats

- ½ teaspoon baking powder

- Dash cinnamon and sea salt

- ½ cup cooked quinoa

- 1 cup finely shredded carrots

- 2 tablespoons ground flaxseed

- ½ cup almond butter

- ¼ cup coconut oil, melted

- $\frac{1}{2}$ cup maple syrup

- $\frac{1}{2}$ cup nuts and/or seeds

- $\frac{1}{2}$ cup dried cranberries

Instructions

Use a food processor to process the $1\frac{1}{4}$ cups rolled oats. In a large bowl, stir together the flour, the remaining 1 cup whole oats, baking powder, baking soda, cinnamon, and sea salt. Fold in the quinoa and then the shredded carrots.

In a small bowl, combine the flaxseed and warm water. In a medium bowl, combine the almond butter, coconut oil, and maple syrup and stir well to incorporate. Stir in the flaxseed mixture.

Add the wet ingredients to the bowl of dry ingredients and fold until just combined. Stir in the walnuts, pepitas, and cranberries.

Scoop onto the baking sheet. Bake for 15 to 18 minutes.

7. Black Bean & Quinoa Snack Bowl

Ingredients

- ¼ cup quinoa(40 g), cooked

- ¼ cup black beans(40 g)

- ¼ cup red onion(35 g), diced

- 2 tablespoons corn

- 1 tablespoon fresh cilantro

- 1 teaspoon lime juice

- salt, to taste

- pepper, to taste

Preparation

Combine all ingredients in a small bowl.

Mix until combined and serve.

Enjoy!

QUINOA SOUPS & STEWS

8. Cream of quinoa mushroom soup

Yield: 4 Servings

Ingredient

- Pam; broth, vinegar or wine for sauteing

- 2 tablespoons Minced shallots

- 8 ounces Mushrooms

- 1 cup Cooked quinoa

- 3 cups Non-fat broth

- $\frac{1}{2}$ cup Evaporated non-fat milk

- Salt and freshly ground black pepper

- $\frac{1}{4}$ cup Chopped fresh dill

Heat the Pam or liquid of choice in a medium saucepan. Cook the shallots until tender. Add the mushrooms, cover and cook for 5 minutes or until tender.

Add the quinoa and broth and bring the liquid to a simmer. Season to taste with salt and pepper and stir in non-fat evaporated milk (or milk substitute). Bring back up to a simmer, remove from heat and stir in the dill. Yield: 4 servings.

9. corn and quinoa chicken soup

Yield: 4 Servings

Ingredient

- 2 cups Water

- 2 cans Low-sodium chicken broth

- ½ cup Quinoa, rinsed

- 2 cups Cooked chicken, diced

- 4 cups Spinach, chopped

- 1 cup Whole kernel corn, frozen

- ½ cup Scallions, chopped

- Salt and pepper

- Hot pepper sauce

In a 3-quart saucepan, bring chicken broth and 2 cups water to boil over high heat. Stir in quinoa and cooked chicken; simmer, covered, 15 minutes.

Add spinach, corn and scallions; return to boiling. Reduce heat; simmer 4 to 5 minutes. Season to taste with salt, pepper and hot pepper sauce.

10.   Tomato lentil stew over quinoa

Yield: 1 servings

Ingredient

- 2 cups Lentils ; washed and boiled

- 2 cups Quinoa ; rinsed and boiled

- 2 larges Onions

- 5 mediums Tomatoes

- 3 tablespoons Canola oil

- $\frac{3}{4}$ teaspoon Salt

- $1\frac{1}{2}$ teaspoon Marjoram

- 1½ teaspoon Savory

In a very large skillet or pan, sautee onions . Add tomatoes and stir occasionally. Crush the marjoram and savory and add to the pan. Add the salt. add the cooked, well drained lentils.Add quinoa.

In a small pan heat some oil and add a couple cloves of chopped or pressed garlic, and a very small amount of diced ginger (optional). Add drained and squeezed arame and sautee for a few minutes.

Add soy sauce to taste. When the arame becomes crispy it's ready to eat. Just sprinkle on top of the stew, or any pasta dish for that matter.

11.   Quinoa corn chowder

Yield: 1 Servings

Ingredient

- ½ cup Quinoa, cooked

- 1 cup Potato, cubed

- 2 Carrots

- 2 smalls Onions

- 3 cups Corn -- can be part creamed

- 2 cups Milk

- 1½ teaspoon Salt

- Fresh ground black pepper

- $\frac{1}{2}$ cup Parsley

- Butter

Simmer quinoa, potato, carrot, celery onion until tender (About 15 min).

Add corn. Bring back to boil and simmer another 5 minutes or so. Add Milk.

Bring jujst to boil. Season to taste. Garnish with parsley and dab of butter.

12.   Saffron quinoa & beet salad

Yield: 6 servings

Ingredient

- 6 tablespoons Extra-virgin olive oil

- 2 tablespoons Fresh lemon juice

- 2 smalls Cloves garlic; minced

- $\frac{1}{2}$ teaspoon Coarse salt

- $\frac{1}{2}$ teaspoon Ground cumin

- $\frac{1}{4}$ teaspoon Red pepper flakes

- 4 smalls Beets with greens attached

- 1 cup quinoa cooked with saffron

- 2 cups Vegetable broth

- 5 teaspoons Olive oil

- 2 ounces Thinly sliced shallots

- 3 mediums Clove garlic; minced

- $1\frac{1}{2}$ tablespoon Fresh lemon juice

- $\frac{1}{4}$ teaspoon Salt

Wrap each beet individually in foil and bake until tender when pierced with thin knife, 45 minutes to 1 hour. Peel and Place beets in small bowl, add 2 to 3 tablespoons of marinade and toss gently.add quinoa

heat 3 teaspoons olive oil over medium-high heat. Add shallots and cook until crisp, stirring often, about 3 minutes. Add garlic and Add beet greens. Stir in lemon juice and salt. Season with pepper.

13.   Black bean and quinoa salad

Ingredient

- 5 tablespoons Olive oil

- ½ cup Quinoa; rinsed

- 1 cup Chicken or vegetable broth

- ¼ teaspoon Ground cumin

- 2 tablespoons Lime juice

- 1 cup Cooked or canned black beans

- 1 cup Whole-kernel corn

- 1 large Ripe tomato

- 1 small Sweet red pepper

- 2 Green onions; finely chopped

- 3 tablespoons Chopped cilantro leaves

- 2 cups Mixed salad greens

heat 1 tablespoon oil over medium heat. Add quinoa and stir until toasted and aromatic-- about 5 minutes. Stir in broth, cumin, and salt; heat to boiling over high heat. Reduce heat to low, cover, and simmer until liquid is absorbed--about 15 minutes.

In medium-size bowl, whisk together remaining 4 tablespoons oil, the lime juice, and black pepper. Stir in black beans, corn, tomato, red pepper, green onions, cilantro, chopped parsley, and cooked quinoa.

To serve, divide greens among 4 salad plates. Spoon quinoa mixture onto greens.

14. Citrus quinoa salad

Yield: 4 Servings

Ingredient

- 1 cup Quinoa, cooked
- 1 cup Diced (unpeeled) cucumber
- ½ cup Diced figs or dried apricots
- ½ cup Mandarin orange sections
- ¼ cup Sunflower seeds
- 2 Green onions; diced
- 2 tablespoons Chopped fresh coriander
- 1 teaspoon Grated lemon or lime rind

- 3 tablespoons Lemon or lime juice

- 3 drops Sesame oil; more or less

- 1 teaspoon Granulated sugar

- $\frac{1}{4}$ teaspoon Ground cumin

- $\frac{1}{4}$ teaspoon Ground coriander

In salad bowl, combine quinoa, cucumber, figs, orange sections, sunflower seeds, onions and coriander.

Dressing: In small bowl, mix lemon rind and juice, sesame oil, sugar, cumin and coriander; pour over salad and toss to mix. Serve immediately or cover and refrigerate for up to 3 days.

15.   Amaranth & quinoa salad

Yield: 4 servings

Ingredient

- 1 cup Quinoa, cooked

- 1 tablespoon Vegetable oil

- Dill Dressing

- 1 tablespoon Amaranth

- 6 smalls Red radishes, sliced

- 1 small Cucumber

- $\frac{1}{4}$ pounds Jarlsberg cheese

- Fresh dill sprigs (opt.)

To pop amaranth, use a small heavy saucepan. Heat the dry saucepan until very hot over medium-high heat. Using a small pastry brush to keep the seeds moving and keep them from burning, add the amaranth and immediately stir and cook until the seeds pop.

Add Dill Dressing, radishes, cucumber, and cheese to cooled quinoa in large bowl. Toss amaranth into the salad. Transfer salad to serving bowl.

Dill Dressing: In jar with tight-fitting lid, combine ⅓C olive oil, 1 t finely grated lemon rind, 2 T lemon juice, 1 T finely chopped fresh dill, 1 T Dijon-style prepared mustard, ½ t salt, and ¼ t ground white pepper. Cover and shake until well mixed.

16.   Eggplant with quinoa

Yield: 4 Servings

Ingredient

- 2 Eggplants, boiled

- 1 cup Quinoa, cooked

- 1 small Onion

- 2 Garlic cloves; minced

- 1 Poblano pepper

- 1 Banana or hungarian pepper

- ½ cup Tomato puree or tomato sauce

- Fresh pepper and salt to taste

- $\frac{1}{4}$ cup Ground walnuts

- 1 cup Cooked chickpeas

- Pinch Wheat flour and Gluten flour

Chop the eggplant insides and set aside to saute.

In a large frying pan, add the water and heat over medium heat. Then add the onion, garlic, peppers, and the eggplant insides, and saute, adding a little more water as needed. Then add the tomato puree, salt, pepper, walnuts, and chickpeas. Cover and simmer about 5 minutes, stirring occasionally. Add the cooked quinoa, wheat flour, and gluten flour to the vegetable saute and stir well. Fill the eggplant shells with the quinoa mixture. Bake.

17. Quinoa summer salad

Yield: 1 recipe

Ingredient

- 4 cups Cooked AM Quinoa
- ½ cup Shelled pecans
- ½ cup Chopped green onion
- ½ cup Sliced black olives
- ¾ cup Sliced mushrooms
- ¾ cup Raisins plumped in hot water
- ¼ cup Lemon juice

- 2 tablespoons Tamari

- ⅓cup Unrefined Olive Oil

- $\frac{1}{4}$ teaspoon Pepper

Mix first six ingredients together in a large bowl. In a separate container mix the last four ingredients. Pour the liquids over the salad and toss gently. For the best flavor let set in the refrigerator for about one hour before serving.

18. Quinoa with tempeh nuggets

Yield: 1 servings

Ingredient

- 1½ cup Quinoa, cooked
- 1½ cup Fresh or frozen corn kernels;
- Tempeh Adobo Nuggets
- 1 cup Red bell pepper; finely diced
- ½ cup Red onion; finely diced
- ½ cup Cilantro; tightly packed, minced
- 1 Jalapeno pepper; seeded, finely diced
- ¼ cup Lime-Shoyu Vinaigrette

- 2 tablespoons Fresh lime juice

- Radicchio; for garnish

Add the corn to quinoa and cook until tender but still crunchy.

When the quinoa stops giving off steam, toss in the tempeh nuggets, red bell pepper, onion, cilantro, jalapeno, and enough vinaigrette to coat the ingredients lightly. Add the lime juice to taste, is desired. Serve warm or at room temperature on a bed of radicchio.

19. Quinoa tabouli salad

Yield: 10 Servings

Ingredient

- 2 cups Quinoa; rinsed
- ¾ cup Fresh parsley, chopped
- ¾ cup Ripe tomatoes; diced
- 1 Cucumber; peeled seeded & diced
- 1 bunch Green onions; chopped
- 5 Sprigs fresh mint; chopped
- 4 tablespoons Extra Virgin Olive Oil
- 2 tablespoons Plum Vinegar
- 2 Garlic cloves peeled and pressed

Cook Quinoa according to package directions. Cool. Combine Quinoa, parsley, tomatoes, cucumbers, garlic, green onions, and mint. Mix well. Combine olive oil, ume plum vinegar and garlic and mix into salad.

20. Ensalada con quinoa

Yield: 7 Servings

Ingredient

- 2 cups cooked Quinoa
- ⅓cup Lime Juice
- 2 Aji chiles
- ⅔cup Olive Oil
- 2 mediums Cucumbers
- 1 large Tomato; seeds removed, cubed
- 8 Green Onions; white only thinly sliced
- ⅓cup Italian Parsley;fresh, mince
- ⅓cup Mint; fresh minced

- Salt and Black Pepper

- 2 Heads of Bibb Lettuce;shred

- 3 Eggs;hard boiled,slice thin

- 2 Fresh Ears of Corn

- 1 cup Black Olives; thickly sliced

Whisk together the lime juice, the chiles, and the olive oil and set aside.

Combine the quinoa, cucumbers, tomato, green onions, parsley, and mint and mix gently. Pour the lime juice mixture over the top and toss again. add salt and freshly ground black pepper to taste.

To serve the salad, place a mound of shredded Bibb lettuce on 6 or 8 individual plates and garnish with any or all of the suggested garnishes.

21.   Fennel quinoa salad

Yield: 1 Servings

Ingredient

- 3 cups Cooked Quinoa

- 1 cup Chopped fennel bulb

- 2 tablespoons Minced shallots

- 1 teaspoon Grated lemon rind

- 1 teaspoon Grated orange rind

- ⅔cup Fresh orange juice

- 2 tablespoons Fresh lemon juice

- ¼ cup Chopped fresh basil

- 2 teaspoons Olive oil
- $\frac{1}{4}$ teaspoon Salt
- $\frac{1}{8}$ teaspoon Pepper
- 2 cups Orange sections
- $\frac{1}{4}$ cup Chopped walnuts, toasted

Combine quinoa, fennel, and shallots in a large bowl; set aside. In a small bowl combine next 8 ingredients(lemon rind thru pepper); stir well. Pour over quinoa mixture and toss well. Spoon 1 cup salad onto each of four plates. Arrange $\frac{1}{2}$ cup orange sections around each salad; sprinkle each salad with 1 Tablespoon walnuts.

22.   Rio grande quinoa salad

Yield: 4 servings

Ingredient

- 3 tablespoons Lemon juice

- 3 tablespoons Olive oil

- 3 tablespoons Cilantro, minced

- Sea salt

- Freshly ground black pepper

- 1 cup Fresh or frozen corn

- $\frac{1}{2}$ cup Quinoa, cooked with cumin

- 1 cup Cooked black beans

- 1 medium Tomato; diced

- 3 tablespoons Red onion, minced

Whisk together lemon juice, olive oil, cilantro, and salt and pepper to taste; set aside.

In a small saucepan, bring 1-$\frac{1}{2}$ cups water to a boil and add corn.

Reduce heat and let corn simmer until tender. Drain corn, reserving 1 cup of cooking liquid.

In a bowl, combine cooled quinoa, corn, black beans, tomato and onion. Pour dressing over and toss gently to mix. Refrigerate salad until ready to serve

23.   Fruited quinoa salad

Yield: 4 Servings

Ingredient

- 3 cups Quinoa, cooked
- $8\frac{3}{4}$ ounce Can apricot halves, drained
- 1 Naval orange, sectioned
- 1 cup Seedless red grapes, halved
- $\frac{1}{4}$ cup Scallions, sliced
- $\frac{1}{4}$ cup Fresh parsley, chopped
- $\frac{1}{4}$ teaspoon Black pepper
- Salt

In a medium bowl, toss quinoa, apricots, oranges, grapes, scallions, parsley and black pepper. Season to taste with salt, if desired.

24.   Herbed quinoa salad

Yield: 4 Servings

Ingredient

- 1½ cup Peas or snap beans

- 3 cups Cold, cooked quinoa-See note

- ½ cup Crumbled low-fat goat cheese

- ⅓cup Chopped fresh parsley

- ⅓cup Chopped fresh tarragon

- ⅓cup Snipped fresh chives

- ⅓cup Lemon juice

- 1 tablespoon Extra-virgin olive oil

In a 2-quart saucepan over high heat, bring one quart water to a boil. Add the peas. Cook for about 4 minutes, or until tender; do not overcook. Drain and rinse under cold water.

Place the quinoa in a large bowl. Add the peas, goat cheese, parsley, tarragon and chives. Toss lightly.

In a cup, whisk together the lemon juice and olive oil. Pour over the salad. Note: To cook the quinoa, bring 2 cups of water or stock to a boil in a 2- quart saucepan. Add 1 cup of quinoa.

Reduce the heat to low, cover the pan and cook for 10-15 minutes, or until tender but not mushy. Drain off any remaining liquid. Fluff with a fork to separate the grains. Allow to cool before combining in salad.

25.   Jicama-quinoa salad

Ingredient

- 4 ounces Sugar snap peas

- 1 pounds Jicama; peeled and

- ½ cup Fresh orange juice

- 1 tablespoon Fresh lemon juice

- 1 tablespoon brown rice vinegar

- ½ teaspoon Coarse salt

- 12 Cherry and/or yellow pear tomatoes

- 1½ cup Cooked quinoa

- ½ cup Chopped fresh cilantro

- 2 Pinches cayenne or dashes hot sauce

Bring small saucepan of water to boil. Add sugar snap peas and cook 1 minute. Drain, rinse under cold running water until cool and drain again.

Cut in half crosswise on the diagonal. Set aside.

In large bowl, combine jicama, orange and lemon juices, vinegar and salt and toss to combine. Add sugar snap peas, cherry tomatoes, quinoa, cilantro and cayenne. Toss gently but thoroughly to combine, Adjust seasoning to taste and serve.

26.　Minted quinoa fruit salad

Yield: 4 Servings

Ingredient

- ¼ teaspoon Salt

- 6 ounces Quinoa; uncooked

- ⅓cup Mint; chopped

- ¼ cup Yogurt

- 2 tablespoons Orange Juice

- 1½ cup Strawberries; sliced

- 2 mediums Kiwi Fruit

- 1 cup Mandarin Oranges

In a medium saucepan, bring 2 cups water and the salt to a boil; add quinoa. Reduce the heat to low; simmer 15 minutes, until quinoa is translucent. In a food processor or blender, combine mint, yogurt and juice, puree until smooth. Set aside.

Set aside six strawberry slices and three kiwi slices for garnish. In large serving bowl, combine the remaining strawberries, the remaining kiwi and the mandarin orange sections. Pour yogurt sauce over fruit mixture; toss to coat. Add cooked quinoa; toss gently to mix well.

Garnish with reserved strawberry and kiwi slices. Refrigerate, covered 1-2 hours, until thoroughly chilled.

Yield: 6 servings

Ingredient

- 3 large Oranges

- 1 cup Baby carrots; sliced thin

- 2 cups Cooked quinoa; millet, or other

- 6 Stalks celery; sliced thin

- ¼ cup honey mustard dressing

- 3 tablespoons Fresh lime juice

- ¼ cup Chopped fresh mint

- Romaine or other lettuce leaves

Combine all ingredients except the lettuce leaves in a serving bowl. Serve the salad on a bed of lettuce, or chop the lettuce and toss it with the salad before serving.

28. Quinoa and shrimp salad

Yield: 4 servings

Ingredient

- 1 cup Quinoa, cooked

- $\frac{1}{2}$ pounds Shrimp; cooked; in 1/2-inch dice

- $\frac{1}{2}$ cup Fresh Coriander; finely chopped

- $\frac{1}{4}$ cup Fresh Chives or Green Onions

- 1 each Jalapeno Pepper; minced

- 1 each Garlic Clove; minced

- 1 teaspoon Salt

- $\frac{1}{2}$ teaspoon Black Pepper

- 3 tablespoons Lime Juice

- 1 tablespoon Honey

- 1 tablespoon Soy Sauce

- 2 tablespoons Olive Oil

Quinoa (pronounced kween wa) is an ancient South American garin that's a complete protein, healthful and delicious. You can use rice or couscous in its place. Serve this as an appetizer or light main course.

For the dressing, whisk together jalapeno, garlic, salt, pepper, lime juice, honey, soy sauce and olive oil. Toss gently with quinoa. Adjust seasoning to taste.

29.   Quinoa en salpicon

Yield: 1 batch

Ingredient

- 2 cups cooked quinoa

- 8 cups ;Water

- 1 cup Peeled, seeded cucumber diced

- 1 cup Seeded and diced tomato

- $\frac{1}{4}$ cup Fresh lime juice

- $\frac{1}{4}$ teaspoon Ground white pepper

- 1 Fresh chile; seeded & minced

- $\frac{1}{2}$ cup Finely sliced scallions

- ⅓cup Chopped fresh Italian parsley

- ⅓cup Chopped fresh mint leaves

- 1 teaspoon Coarse salt

- ½ cup Olive oil

In a bowl, whisk together the lime juice, pepper, chile and salt. Gradually add the olive oil, stirring constantly. Set aside.

When the grain has cooled, assemble the salad. In a bowl place the quinoa with the cucumber, tomato, scallions, parsley and mint. Toss to mix the ingredients, then add the vinaigrette and toss thoroughly.

Season to taste with salt and white pepper

30.   Quinoa fiesta salad

Yield: 1 Serving

Ingredient

- 1 cup Quinoa, cooked

- 2 cups Water

- 1 Red pepper; cored, seeded, and diced

- 1 carrot

- 6 Scallions

- ¼ cup Cooked corn

- ½ cup Currants

- 2 tablespoons Fresh parsley

- 1 Clove garlic; peeled and minced

- 1 teaspoon Cumin

- 2 tablespoons Maple syrup

- 1 tablespoon Fresh lemon juice

- 1 tablespoon Rice vinegar

- 2 tablespoons Raspberry vinegar

Sauté the garlic in sauté liquid of choice for 2 minutes. Add the cumin and sauté another minute. Add sweetener, stir to melt, remove from heat, and allow cooling. Add lemon juice and vinegars. Mix well and pour onto quinoa, along with the vegetables, parsley, and currants.

Mix gently but thoroughly. Serve immediately or place in the refrigerator to chill. Serve on a bed of greens.

31. Quinoa mandarin salad

Yield: 1 Serving

Ingredient

- 1 cup cooked quinoa

- 1 can mandarin orange

- 6 Oz; (2 cups) fresh snow pea pods

- ⅓cup Sliced green onions

- Leaf Lettuce leaves

- 1 tablespoon Honey

- ¼ teaspoon Salt

- 3 tablespoons Apple cider vinegar

- 2 tablespoons Canola oil

- $\frac{1}{8}$ teaspoon Hot pepper flakes

In a medium saucepan, combine quinoa and orange liquid mixture. Stir in pea pods and onions. Cool 10 minutes.

Meanwhile, in small jar with tight-fitting lid, combine all dressing ingredients, shake well. Refrigerate until serving time.

In med. bowl, combine quinoa mixture and mandarin orange segments. Cover; refrigerate at least 1 hour or until chilled.

Just before serving, line 4 individual salad plates with lettuce. Pour dressing over salad, stir gently to coat. Spoon salad onto lettuce-line plates. 4 (1-$\frac{1}{2}$ cup) servings

32. Quinoa olive medley

Yield: 8 Servings

Ingredient

- 2 cups Eden Quinoa; rinsed
- ⅔cup Black olives; cut in half
- ⅔cup Green olives; cut in half
- ¼ cup Pine nuts; lightly roasted
- 1 bunch Green onions; finely chopped
- ¼ cup Parsley; finely chopped
- ½ small Red pepper cut into thin strips

- 2 Garlic cloves; finely minced

- 2 tablespoons Extra Virgin Olive Oil

- 4 tablespoons Plum Vinegar

Cook Quinoa according to package directions. Cool, then mix in remaining ingredients, adding Ume Vinegar last and seasoning to taste. Delicious as a salad or side dish

33. Quinoa stuffed onions

Yield: 6 servings

Ingredient

- 12 mediums Onions; peeled
- ½ cup Quinoa; cooked
- 1 cup ;water
- ¼ teaspoon Sea salt
- 2 Garlic cloves; minced (opt)
- ½ cup Mushrooms; sliced
- ½ cup Celery; sliced
- 2 tablespoons Corn or olive oil

- $\frac{1}{2}$ cup Chickpeas; cooked
- 1 cup Walnuts; roasted
- 2 teaspoons Soy sauce
- 2 teaspoons Brown rice vinegar

Hollow out insides of onions with an apple corer, leaving bottoms intact and reserving insides. Steam hollowed-out onions until tender, reserving $\frac{3}{4}$ cup of cooking liquid.

Finely chop reserved onions. Sauté chopped onions, garlic, mushrooms and celery in oil for 15 minutes or until soft. Mix in quinoa and chickpeas and heat through (about 5 minutes).

Fill onions with quinoa mixture. Crush walnuts in a food processor blending in soy sauce and vinegar to form a creamy mixture. Blend in reserved cooking liquid. Place mixture in a saucepan and heat through, stirring constantly. Pour over stuffed onions, garnish and serve.

34.   Tomatoes stuffed with quinoa

Yield: 4 Servings

Ingredient

- 4 Beefsteak tomatoes

- Salt

- 2 cups Cooked quinoa

- 2 Kirby (pickling) cucumbers;

- ⅓cup Chopped fresh parsley

- ⅓cup Chopped fresh mint

- 2 Scallions; finely sliced

- $\frac{1}{4}$ cup Broth

- 2 tablespoons Fresh lime juice

- Fresh Jalapeno pepperr

Salt the insides of the hollowed out tomatoes and drain them upside down on a rack. In a mixing bowl combine the quinoa, cucumbers, parsley, herb and scallions. Make a dressing of the broth, lime juice, jalapeno pepper and toss with the vegetables and quinoa. Season to taste with salt and pepper.

Stuff tomatoes with the salad and serve one tomato to each person.

QUINOA DESSERTS

35. Creamy quinoa pudding

Yield: 4 Servings

Ingredient

- 1 cup Quinoa; rinsed

- 2½ cup Eden soy

- ⅛ teaspoon Sea Salt

- 1 teaspoon,Sesame butter or tahini

- 2 tablespoons Barley Malt Syrup

- 2 tablespoons Kudzu; dissolved in...

- 2 tablespoons Cold water

- 1 tablespoon Vanilla

- $\frac{1}{2}$ teaspoon Fresh grated nutmeg

Put Quinoa, Eden soy and salt in a saucepan and bring to a boil. Cover and simmer for 20 minutes. Add sesame butter and Barley Malt Syrup.

Mix well. Add Kudzu, stirring constantly until mixture thickens. Add vanilla and spices. Top with your choice of nuts or fruit. Delicious warm or chilled

36.   Quinoa dessert pudding

Yield: 1 serving

Ingredient

- ½ cup Raisins

- ½ cup Dark rum

- 2 cups Quinoa; rinsed, well drained

- 2 cups Whole milk

- 1⅓cup Whipping cream

- 1⅓cup Sugar

- ½ teaspoon Salt

- 1 teaspoon Ground cinnamon

- $\frac{1}{4}$ teaspoon Ground nutmeg

- 3 large Egg yolks

- Additional ground cinnamon; for garnish

Combine raisins and rum in pot. Bring to boil. Remove from heat. Set aside to plump. Cook quinoa in large pot of boiling water until tender. Drain well. Combine quinoa, milk, cream, sugar, salt, cinnamon and nutmeg in heavy large saucepan over medium heat. Bring to boil, stirring frequently.

Reduce heat to low. Cook until most of liquid evaporates and mixture is thick, stirring frequently, about 15 minutes. Whisk egg yolks in large bowl to blend. Add 1 cup pudding mixture and whisk to blend. Return mixture to saucepan. Add raisins and rum and continue stirring until mixture is thick (do not boil). Transfer pudding to large glass bowl. Refrigerate until cool. Sprinkle with cinnamon before serving.

37.   Quinoa with toasted hazelnuts

Yield: 1 serving

Ingredient

- 1 tablespoon Olive oil

- 1 small Onion; finely chopped

- 1 cup Quinoa; rinsed well in

- Cold water

- 2 cups Chicken stock

- 1 Bay leaf

- 1 tablespoon Cinnamon

- $\frac{1}{2}$ cup Dried cranberries

- $\frac{1}{2}$ teaspoon Salt

- $\frac{1}{2}$ teaspoon black pepper

- $\frac{1}{2}$ cup Sliced hazelnuts

- 2 tablespoons Butter

In a small saucepan, heat the oil for 1 minute before adding the diced onion. Sweat the onion until it wilts, stir in the quinoa and toast the grains for 1 minute before adding the chicken stock. Bring the stock to the boil, lower the heat to a simmer, add the bay leaf, cinnamon, cranberries, salt and pepper and cook for 15 minutes until all the liquid is absorbed.

At the end of the cooking time, stir in the nuts and butter, cover the pan and let sit for 5 minutes before serving.

38. Sweet potato-quinoa cakes

Yield: 18 servings

Ingredient

- 1 large Egg
- 2 Egg whites
- 3 cups Cooked quinoa
- 2 cups Peeled; grated sweet potato
- 2 bunches Thinly sliced scallions
- 1 bunch Finely chopped cilantro
- ½ cup Quinoa flour
- 2 teaspoons Coarse salt

- $\frac{1}{2}$ teaspoon ground black pepper

- Vegetable oil for frying

- Lime wedges for garnish

In large bowl, lightly beat egg and egg whites. Add quinoa, sweet potato, scallions, cilantro, quinoa flour, salt and pepper and mix well. Let stand 15 minutes.

In large skillet, heat 2 teaspoons vegetable oil over medium-high heat until hot but not smoking. Cook cakes in batches, using about $\frac{1}{4}$ cup of quinoa mixture for each cake and flattening slightly with back of spoon to form a 3-inch disk. Cook until golden brown, about 3 minutes per side, reducing heat if cakes brown too quickly.

Drain on paper towels and keep warm in oven. Repeat with remaining cakes, adding more oil to pan as needed. Serve hot with lime wedges to squeeze over cakes.

Chocolate Quinoa Pudding

Ingredients:

- 1/2 cup cooked quinoa

- 1/2 tsp vanilla extract

- 1/2 cup cocoa powder (or raw cacao powder)

- 1/2 cup almond milk (or coconut milk)

- 1 tbsp brown sugar

Instructions:

Combine all the ingredients in a bowl and mix

Refrigerate for at least a couple of hours

Serve and enjoy!

40.   Apple Pie Quinoa Parfait

- 1 cup Greek yogurt

- 1 apple, chopped

- 1/4 cup dry quinoa

- 1/2 tablespoon cinnamon

- 1/2 teaspoon nutmeg

- 1/2 teaspoon salt

- 1 tablespoon brown sugar

Preheat oven to 375.

Combine chopped apple, brown sugar, 1/4 tablespoon cinnamon, 1/4 teaspoon nutmeg and 1/4 teaspoon salt in an oven safe dish. Roast apples until soft and caramelized, about 15-20 minutes.

Combine dry quinoa with remaining cinnamon, nutmeg and salt. Cook according to directions.

When apples and quinoa have cooled (not completely, but they shouldn't be scalding) layer in a glass with Greek yogurt. If desired, mix yogurt with cinnamon and honey for topping.

41.   Chocolate Quinoa Cake

Ingredients

Cake Ingredients:

- 2 cups cooked quinoa loosely packed

- 1/3 cup milk

- 4 eggs

- 1 teaspoon vanilla

- 3/4 cup butter melted

- 1 1/2 cups white sugar

- 1 cup unsweetened cocoa powder

- 1 1/2 teaspoons baking powder

- 1/2 teaspoon baking soda

- 1/2 teaspoon fine sea salt

Frosting Ingredients:

- 2 cups heavy whipping cream

- 1 cup semi-sweet or dark chocolate chips

Instructions

Combine the milk, eggs and vanilla in the blender. Add the cooked quinoa and the butter and puree until completely smooth. Whisk together the dry ingredients in a mixing bowl and add the contents from the blender. Bake on a center oven rack for 28-30 minutes.

Prepare chocolate chips and cream frosting.

42. Quinoa strawberry pudding

INGREDIENTS

- ½ cup Quinoa, cooked

- 2 cups Coconut milk

- 1 cup Water

- 6 Strawberries

- ⅓cup Raw cane sugar

- Pinch of cardamom powder

- 2 tbsp Mixed dry fruits powder

Instructions

Add 1.5 cups of coconut milk to quinoa and cook it for 10 minutes. By now, kheer will be creamy and quinoa is completely cooked.

Add ⅓cup sugar and let it simmer for 5 more minutes.

Switch off the flame and add a pinch of cardamom powder. Mix the kheer well.

Let it cool for some time and add chopped strawberries and dry fruits powder. I have added half more cup of coconut milk to adjust the consistency.

43.   Quinoa Ice Cream Nest

- Unsweetened Soya Drink, Organic 1 Litre

- 200ml Soya Milk.

- Smooth Cashew Nut Butter 1kg

- 6 Tbsp of Cashew Butter.

- Vanilla Paste 100ml

- 2 tsp Vanilla Paste.

- Xanthan Gum 110g

- Corn Flakes, Organic 375g

- 55g of Cornflakes slightly crushed.

- Organic Puffed Quinoa 250g

- 25g of Quinoa Puffs.

- Coconut Blossom Nectar Syrup, 350g

- 6-7 Tbsp of Coconut Nectar Syrup.

- Cuisine Coconut Oil 610ml

- Coco Mylk Chocolate 35g

- 114g of Chocolate

Method

Stir melted chocolate and Coconut Oil and 2 tablespoons of the Coconut Syrup. Add the puffed quinoa and cornflakes.

Spoon the mixture into individual cupcake molds or cases. Create a dip or well and refrigerate.

Blend Soya Milk, Cashew Butter, Vanilla Paste, Xanthan Gum and Coconut Syrup.Freeze.

Spoon the ice-cream into each nest and garnish.

44.   Ricotta and Quinoa Cake

Ingredients:

- 7 ounces bittersweet chocolate

- 5 ounces ricotta cheese

- 6 eggs

- 3 ounces almond flour (or meal)

- 4 tablespoons cooked quinoa

- 4 ounces powdered sugar

Directions:

Melt the chocolate in a double boiler or in the microwave, stirring occasionally.

In a medium-size bowl, mix the melted chocolate into the ricotta.

In a small bowl, gently mix eggs, using a whisk or fork. Add the eggs to the chocolate mixture, followed by the almond flour and the quinoa.

Pour the batter into 4 small ramekins, custard cups or small cake molds. Bake in a preheated 350° F oven for 30 minutes.

Let rest for a few minutes before removing from the molds. Sprinkle with powdered sugar. Serve warm.

45.   Almond Quinoa Blondies

Ingredients

- ¼ cup unsalted butter, softened

- ¾ cup natural almond butter

- 2 large eggs

- ¾ cup packed light brown sugar

- 1 teaspoon vanilla extract

- ¾ cup quinoa flour

- 1 teaspoon baking powder

- ¼ teaspoon salt

- 1 cup semisweet chocolate chips

Directions

Beat butter and almond butter in a mixing bowl with an electric mixer until creamy. Beat in eggs, brown sugar and vanilla. Whisk quinoa flour, baking powder and salt in a small bowl. Mix the flour mixture into the wet ingredients until just combined. Stir in chocolate chips. Spread the batter evenly into the prepared pan.

Bake 25 to 35 minutes.

Baked Quinoa Pudding

Ingredients

- 1 1/2 cups cold water

- 1 cup quinoa, cooked

- 3 large eggs lightly beaten

- 1 1/2 cups low-fat milk

- 1/2 cup half & half

- 1/3 cup agave nectar

- 1 teaspoon vanilla

- 1/2 teaspoon kosher salt

- 1 cup raisins

- 1/2 teaspoon ground cinnamon

- 1/2 teaspoon freshly grated nutmeg

- Agave whipped cream for topping

Instructions

Whisk together the eggs, milk, half & half, agave, vanilla, salt, raisins, cinnamon and nutmeg. Mix the cooled quinoa into the egg mixture. Pour the pudding into a 1 1/2 to 2 quart casserole dish. Make a water bath by placing the pudding-filled baking dish into a larger 4-quart casserole dish that's set on a baking sheet.

Slide the baking sheet with the pans into the oven, and then carefully pour the hot water you've been simmering into the large casserole dish so that hot water reaches halfway up the outside of the pudding dish. Bake for 25 minutes.

Serve warm, topped with whipped cream or vanilla ice cream.

QUINOA SNACKS

47.   Gingered lamb and quinoa

Ingredient

- 1 medium Onion; finely chopped

- 3 ounces Oyster mushrooms

- $\frac{1}{2}$ pounds Lean ground lamb

- $\frac{1}{2}$ teaspoon Fresh thyme leaves

- 3 cups Quinoa; cooked

- $\frac{1}{3}$cup Roasted red peppers

- $\frac{1}{4}$ cup Pine nuts; or less

- 1 tablespoon Fresh ginger root

- 16 Sheets phyllo dough; thawed

Heat oil in a medium sauté pan over medium high heat

Add the onion and sauté for about 4 minutes, or until translucent. Add mushrooms and sauté for about 5 minutes, Add the lamb and sauté for 4 minutes. Season with thyme, sea salt, and freshly ground pepper

Combine the lamb mixture with the quinoa, red pepper, parsley, nuts and ginger.

Unroll the phyllo sheets on a smooth dry surface. Spray each with margarine and layer the prepared sheets one on top of another. Spread with filling and roll.

Bake until golden.

48.   Frituras de quinoa

Yield: 6 Servings

Ingredient

- ⅔cup cooked quinoa

- 1⅓cup Cold water

- ¼ cup All-purpose flour

- 3 tablespoons Parmesan; Grated

- ¾ teaspoon Salt

- ⅛ teaspoon White Pepper; Ground

- 4 Green onions

- 1 large Egg; lightly beaten

- 1 large Egg yolk

- $\frac{3}{4}$ cup Vegetable oil

- Lemon wedges; for serving

In a large bowl, combine the quinoa, flour, Parmesan, salt, and pepper. Mix thoroughly and add the green onions, parsley, egg, and egg yolk. Blend together thoroughly until the mixture has the consistency of a soft dough.

In a large, heavy skillet, heat the oil over medium heat. Using 2 soup spoons, shape the mixture into egg shapes and drop them gently into the hot oil.

Cook, turning over once the croquettes are firm and golden on the bottom, until all the croquettes are golden on all sides (about 1 minute total). Drain briefly on paper towels and serve with lemon wedges.

49.   Quinoa Dessert Bites

Ingredients

- 1 cup Quinoa, cooked

- 1 cup oats, dry

- 1/2 teaspoon cinnamon

- 1/4 teaspoon salt

- 2 tablespoon brown sugar

- 1/2 cup, quartered or chopped apple

- 1/2 cup coconut flakes

- 2 large egg

- 1/2 cup baking chocolate, unsweetened, squares

Instructions

In a large mixing bowl, add your cooked quinoa, oats, and chopped fruit. In a separate smaller mixing bowl, combine your cinnamon, sugar and salt. Add the spice mixture to the quinoa and oats. Stir in your chopped fruit. Once combined add the eggs, and mix just until combined.

Scoop into a sprayed mini muffin tin, making sure the pan is thoroughly sprayed.

Bake for 15-20 minutes, and let cool

Place chocolate squares in a microwave-safe bowl and microwave on low 2-3 minutes until melted.

Dip the dessert bites in chocolate and place on parchment paper to cool.

50.   Quinoa garden cakes

Ingredient

- 1 cup Quinoa, cooked
- 1½ tablespoon Minced red onion
- ½ teaspoon Minced garlic
- ⅔cup Grated carrots
- ⅔cup Grated yellow squash
- 5 ounces Chopped spinach; squeeze dry
- 1 large Lemon; zest of
- 4 tablespoons Unbleached flour
- 1 teaspoon Baking powder
- 1 Egg

- 2 teaspoons Salt

- ½ teaspoon ground black pepper

- 1½ tablespoon Dill; minced

- ½ teaspoon Canola oil

- 1½ cup Nonfat plain yogurt

- 2 teaspoons Fresh lemon juice

Combine all ingredients with the exception of 1 C yogurt, lemon juice, canola oil. Preheat oven to 400 degrees. Rub oil on cookie sheet.

Divide quinoa into 8 balls. Flatten each ball onto cookie sheet to make a 4-inch cake.

Bake 10 minutes, flip cakes over. Bake 10 minutes.

Combine yogurt and lemon juice, serve with cakes.

CONCLUSION

The amount of research on quinoa has grown tremendously over the years, in part because of the hype, but in larger part due to the seed's continually recognized health benefits. The nutrient-rich pseudo-cereal is proposed to reduce the risk of a number of illnesses, and provide an ideal protein-packed substitute for gluten-free diets.

Whole grains like quinoa have been considered preventative for certain types of cancer due to their high levels of fiber. One study from The Journal of Nutrition suggests that the dietary fiber in whole grains may help lower LDL, or "bad," levels of cholesterol, boost digestive health, and potentially lower the risk for some gastrointestinal cancers, such as colon cancer.

Lightning Source UK Ltd.
Milton Keynes UK
UKHW020746250621
386136UK00005B/67